Joseph Alden

Thoughts on the Religious Life

Joseph Alden

Thoughts on the Religious Life

ISBN/EAN: 9783337876982

Printed in Europe, USA, Canada, Australia, Japan

Cover: Foto ©Lupo / pixelio.de

More available books at **www.hansebooks.com**

THOUGHTS

ON

THE RELIGIOUS LIFE

BY

JOSEPH ALDEN, D.D., LL.D.

Author of "The Science of Government," "Studies in Bryant," Etc.

WITH AN INTRODUCTION
BY
WILLIAM CULLEN BRYANT

NEW YORK
G. P. PUTNAM'S SONS
182 FIFTH AVENUE
1879

NOTE.

SOME years since, Mr. Bryant, while conversing with me on the subject of personal religion, was pleased to say that the publication of the views I had expressed would be useful in aiding persons to form a true idea of the religious life. I told him I would write a small book on the subject if he would furnish an introduction to it. He said he thought he would do so, and when subsequently informed that my wife earnestly desired it, he cordially consented.

I told him that the book would not be likely to contain any views which he could not indorse. He replied that he should be sorry if he thought there was any difference in our religious views.

In speaking thus, he had reference to

religion as a life. In our not infrequent conversations on the subject of religion, especially in his season of deep affliction, no reference was ever made to creeds or doctrines except as implied in the expression of personal experience.

Various circumstances prevented me from completing my work till December, 1877. I then sent Mr. Bryant my manuscript, and received from him the following note:

NEW YORK, January 7, 1878.
No. 24 West Sixteenth St.

MY DEAR FRIEND,

I have read your tract very carefully. It is admirably condensed, and gives much in little space. I think I can write a preface to it, but I hope that you are in no hurry for it, as I want time for reflection.

·Yours very truly,
W. C. BRYANT.

At an interview in February, on being asked whether he found in the manuscript anything to which he objected, he replied that there were a few forms of expression which he should not have used. When I proposed to change them if he would point them out, he said that it was unnecessary, as no harm could come from their use.

He mentioned some business matters which required his attention, and would cause some delay in preparing the proposed introduction. At a later interview, he expressed his regret that he had not been able to give his attention to the matter, and the hope that he should be able to do so soon.

In the latter part of May, he informed me that in a few days the proposed work would be done. In this, our last interview, while speaking of the close of life, I asked him whether the sentiment expressed in one of his poems was habitually felt by him. He immediately repeated the passage alluded to—

"Yet these, within my heart
Can neither wake the dread nor the longing to depart,"

and said that the sentiment was habitual. He then with great simplicity and humility expressed his entire reliance upon Christ for salvation. Before many days, he was called to his heavenly home.

The manuscript from which the following introduction is printed, was lying on the table in his study at the time of his decease. By some means it was mislaid, and has just come to hand. It was written, according to Mr. Bryant's habit, on separate pieces of paper, each carefully numbered. Several of the pieces thus numbered cannot be found. This, of course, leaves the essay in a fragmentary condition.

Though fragmentary, it meets the object of the desire alluded to in the first paragraph—that of placing on record Mr. Bryant's testimony to his belief in the gospel of Christ, and his personal interest in its precious truths.

J. A.

ALBANY, January, 1879.

INTRODUCTION.

BY WILLIAM CULLEN BRYANT.

A LADY whom I esteemed and honored in her lifetime, and who is now in heaven, earnestly desired that I should contribute a preface to a treatise by my friend, her husband, on the Religious Life. In doing this, I am paying a duty which I owe to her gentle and Christian memory.

In those respects in which there may exist a divergence of views among Christian denominations, so far as these are touched upon in this work, I desire not to be understood as expressing any opinion. But I will direct the attention of the reader to the beautiful system of devout and holy living which my friend has built upon it, the harmonious manner in which he has portrayed its humility, its self-renunciation, its trust in God, its love of Christ, its purity, its forbearance, its forgiving spirit, its labors for the good of others, and, to use the words of the Apostle, "If there be any virtue, if there be any praise," they are included in the summary of the qualities which form the religious character as conformed to the Christian standard. The author is a close thinker, and has the art of setting forth his thoughts with clearness and simplicity, as well as condensation, and with an avoidance of the theological terms of the schools. So amiable a picture cannot, I am sure, be contemplated without admiration nor without a desire to resemble in reality.

I can only regret that there should be any who, endowed with the same powers of thought and expression, have disowned the humble and simple faith which, carried out into the daily acts of life, produces results so desirable, so important to the welfare of mankind in the present state of existence, and so essential to a preparation for the life upon which we are to enter when we pass beyond the grave.

I cannot but lament the tendency of the time—encouraged by some in the zealous prosecution of science—to turn its attention from the teachings of the gospel, from the beautiful example of Christ's life, and the supremely excellent precepts which he gave to his disciples and the people who resorted to hear him. To those teachings and that example the world owes its recovery from the abominations of heathenism. The very men who, in the pride of their investigations into the secrets of the material world, turn a look of scorn upon the Christian system of belief, are not aware how much of the peace and order of society, how much of the happiness of their households and the purity of those who are dearest to them, are owing to the influence of that religion extending beyond their sphere. There is no character, in the whole range of qualities which distinguish men from each other, so fitted to engage our admiration and so pregnant with salutary influence on society, as that which is formed on the Christian pattern by the precepts of the gospel, and a zealous imitation of the example of the Great Master. If that class should cease to exist, if their example and influence, and the testimony they bear against . . . .

This character, of which Christ was the perfect model, is in itself so attractive, so "altogether lovely," that I cannot describe in language the admiration with which I regard it; nor can I express the gratitude I feel for the dispensation which bestowed that example on mankind, for the truths which he taught and the sufferings he endured for our sakes. I tremble to think what the world would be without Him. Take away the blessing of the advent of his life and the blessings purchased by his death, in what an abyss of guilt would man have been left!

It would seem to be blotting the sun out of the heavens—to leave our system of worlds in chaos, frost, and darkness.

In my view of the life, the teachings, the labors, and the sufferings of the blessed Jesus, there can be no admiration too profound, no love of which the human heart is capable, too warm, no gratitude too earnest and deep of which He is justly the object. It is with sorrow that my love for Him is so cold, and my gratitude so inadequate. It is with sorrow that I see any attempt to put aside His teachings as a delusion, to turn men's eyes from his example, to meet with doubt and denial the story of his life. For my part, if I thought that the religion of skepticism were to gather strength and prevail and become the dominant view of mankind, I should despair of the fate of mankind in the years that are yet to come. . . . .

The religious man finds in his relations to his Maker, a support to his virtue which others cannot have. He acts always with a consciousness that he is immediately under the eye of a Being who looks into his heart and sees his inmost thoughts, and discerns the motives which he is half unwilling to acknowledge even to himself. He feels that he is under the inspection of a Being who is only pleased with right motives and purity of intention, and who is displeased with whatever is otherwise. He feels that the approbation of that Being is infinitely more to be valued than the applause of all mankind, and his displeasure more to be feared and more to be avoided than any disgrace which he might sustain from his brethren of mankind. When, in addition to this consideration, he reflects on the frailty of human virtue, and considers the weakness of his own purposes, it is a . . . .

TABLE OF CONTENTS.

CHAPTER I.
The True Idea of the Religious Life.............. 15

CHAPTER II.
The Religious Life Desirable..................... 23

CHAPTER III.
Entrance on the Religious Life.................. 29

CHAPTER IV.
Notice of Some Errors........................... 37

CHAPTER V.
Penitence....................................... 42

CHAPTER VI.
How to Repent.................................. 50

CHAPTER VII.
The True Idea of Faith.......................... 56

CHAPTER VIII.
The Religious Life Progressive.................. 63

CHAPTER IX.
Justice and Mercy............................... 68

CHAPTER X.
Prayer.................................... 75

CHAPTER XI.
Influence of the Spirit..................... 81

CHAPTER XII.
Meditation.—Secret Prayer................. 87

CHAPTER XIII.
Doing Good................................ 92

CHAPTER XIV.
Justice.—Sympathy.—Self-denial.—Cross-bearing.... 97

CHAPTER XV.
Religious Conversation.—Social Worship........... 103

CHAPTER XVI.
Intelligence.—Courtesy....................... 108

CHAPTER XVII.
Religious Emotion.—Zeal..................... 112

CHAPTER XVIII.
Vain Speculation............................ 115

CHAPTER XIX.
Conformity to the World.—Preparation for Heaven.. 119

THOUGHTS ON THE RELIGIOUS LIFE.

CHAPTER I.

THE TRUE IDEA OF THE RELIGIOUS LIFE.

MAN has the capacity of seeing by means of the eye. Without light and visible objects, this capacity would be valueless. Light and objects are furnished him.

Man has the capacity of knowing and of seeing that which is right—duty. Duties are set before him. Man's capacities are furnished with corresponding objects.

Man has capacities for love, reverence, and obedience. An object perfectly adapted to these capacities is found in God. We have the same reason to believe that man was made to love, reverence, and obey God, which we have to believe that he was made to see visible objects.

All persons who admit the existence of an all-wise, omnipotent, holy Creator of men, admit that His will ought to be done by men. His will is wise and right. Man was made to do what is wise and right.

A wise man is one who acts in accordance with the dictates of wisdom. A benevolent man is one who acts in accordance with the dictates of benevolence. A religious man is one who acts in accordance with the will of God. As the Bible is the word of God, a man is religious in proportion to his obedience to the requirements of the Bible.

The will of God has respect to all the actions of men, at all times, and under all circumstances. It is God's will that men be industrious; that they take care of their health; that they be honest, truthful, benevolent; that they be thankful for favors, and penitent for sin; that they have faith in God. They can never be placed in circumstances where the will of God has no relation to them. It is always to be their guide. Men are religious so far as they follow this guide.

This view of the religious life differs from that entertained by many persons. They make a distinction between the religious and the secular life. The actions ascribed to the latter—the labors of the farmer, the artisan, the lawyer—have, in their view, a moral, but not a religious character. Acts of prayer, of public worship, of self-denial, efforts for the extension of the church, have, in their view, a religious character.

If this distinction be correct, a man may be a very religious man, while his conduct in the secular life may not be very commendable. He may be constant in attending the prayer meeting; but not careful to pay his just debts. He may be very zealous for the conversion of souls; but not strictly accurate in his statements in regard to worldly matters. He may be abundant in labors at a protracted meeting; while a piece of work which he has promised to do for a neighbor remains undone.

It is God's will that a man should pray; it is also His will that a man should pay his debts. To pay one's debts is as truly a religious duty as to pray. To speak the exact truth is as truly a religious duty as to exhort men to flee from the wrath to come. To meet one's just engagements is as truly a religious duty as to attend the public worship of God. God's will has reference to all the actions of men. Hence, there is no ground for making a distinction between the secular and religious life. The whole of life should be religious. Man has but one thing to do—his duty to God.

Writers divide man's duties into those which he owes to himself, those which he owes to his fellow men, and those which he owes to God. Man owes it to himself to take care of his health. It is God's will that he should take care of his health. It is man's duty to his neighbor to deal honestly with him. It is God's will that he should deal honestly with his neighbor. To be honest is as truly a religious duty as to be devout.

A distinction may be made between morality and religion—between a moral and a religious life. A moral man is one who avoids the practice of vice, and does to his fellow men what they may require of him. A man may be a moral man without being a religious man. He may avoid the practice of vice, and perform his duties toward his fellow men, without reference to the will of God—without believing in the existence of God. An atheist may be a moral man.

It may be asked: "If a man is a religious man in proportion as he does the will of God, is not the atheist who speaks the truth, and who is honest and benevolent, so far forth a religious man?"

He is not; for, in his actions he has no reference to the will of God. To do, without reference to the will of God, what God requires, is not obeying Him.

Let it be understood, then, that a religious life is a life of obedience to the will of God—a life spent in the service of God. A true idea of the religious life is a necessary condition of wise efforts toward its realization.

It may be objected that this view of the religious life makes religion to consist wholly in action, and gives no place to feeling. In the view of many persons, religion consists chiefly in feeling.

God has given man capacities for knowing, feeling, and willing. These capacities are to be exercised in accordance with the will of God. Man's varied feelings form a very important portion of his life. His feelings give character to his actions. God's will has reference to man's feelings as well as to his volitions or actions. All his emotions desires, affections, and passions—all the exercises of his emotive nature must be in accordance with the will of God. The Bible gives due prominence to man's emotive nature.

"I desire religion that I may be happy," says one. This indicates the idea entertained by many, that religion is something which makes its possessor happy, and is therefore desirable.

Religion is not a possession, but a life—a life regulated by the will of God. There is no such thing as religion apart from a religious life. To seek for religion is to seek for conformity to the will of God. Perfect conformity to the will of God is perfect holiness. Holiness is the great object of the religious life. We are to seek holiness, not because we shall gain happiness thereby, but because it is right.

God has ordained that right doing shall be followed by happiness. Happiness is not something to be possessed. It is a condition of soul consequent upon the performance of duty.

Happiness is closely connected with the

exercise of the emotive nature. God requires the exercise most conducive to happiness. Man's highest happiness is found in the exercise of love. To love God with all the heart is to be as happy as the constitution of our nature will allow. A man is happy just in proportion as he is religious. As God is infinitely wise, his precepts must be the best possible precepts. The best possible precepts must tend to the perfection of the soul. The highest possible perfection can be attained by obeying God—by becoming a religious man.

CHAPTER II.

THE RELIGIOUS LIFE DESIRABLE.

SOME things, undesirable in themselves, are the necessary means to desirable ends. Some persons take this view of the religious life. They regard it as something to be endured for the sake of the advantages which it secures.

The religious life is desirable in itself. It is desirable that the soul should put forth its true life, just as it is desirable that the tree should put forth its true life.

In becoming religious, a man becomes what God made him to be. It is desirable that man should be what the all-wise and benevolent Creator made him to be.

It is desirable that the child should be in sympathy with his loving parent. God teaches us to call him our Father. He always teaches us that which is true. He is a just and loving Father. His children ought to be in sympathy with him. It is unseemly for the child to be indifferent to the interest and affection of his loving Father.

We all know the connection between love and happiness. Our highest happiness consists in the exercise of affection toward worthy objects. The purer the affection, and the more perfect the object, the greater the happiness.

The religious life is a life of love, of obedience prompted by love. Hence, love is said to be the fulfilling of the law.

Acts prompted by love are always happy acts. The tendency of religion is to make every act of our lives a happy act. So far from interfering with man's happiness, religion makes the fullest provision for it.

It is desirable to be in sympathy with God as the omnipotent Ruler. God governs the universe. He doeth his will in the armies of heaven, and among the inhabitants of the earth. He worketh all things according to the counsel of his own will. None can strengthen himself against him and prosper.

It is certainly desirable to have the favor and protection of the omnipotent Ruler. In no other way can man accomplish the objects he was made to accomplish. In no other way can he be successful in his lifework.

No man expects to succeed in opposition to God's physical laws. No man expects to rear a stable column whose line of gravity falls without the base. No man expects to make a successful voyage in a vessel whose specific gravity is greater than that of water.

God's moral laws are more unchangeable than his physical laws. Heaven and earth shall pass away sooner than one jot or one tittle of the law shall fail. God can suspend the law of gravitation; but he cannot suspend the law of holiness. And yet men expect to succeed while disregarding God's moral law!

It may be said: "They do succeed—they gain wealth, pleasure, power."

A man does not succeed in crossing the ocean when he gets halfway over and goes to the bottom. The success of an immortal being must have reference to the whole duration of his being. He who succeeds in his plans for a few years, and fails for the remaining years of his life, cannot be called a successful man. He who succeeds for threescore years and ten, and fails for eternity, cannot be called a successful man. As all plans in opposition to the laws of gravitation must ultimately fail, so all plans in opposition to the law of holiness must ultimately fail.

The dictates of holiness are coincident with the dictates of infinite wisdom. Efforts put forth in accordance with the dictates of infinite wisdom, cannot fail. They will accomplish just what infinite wisdom designs they shall accomplish. Let a man follow God's directions, and his labors will not be in vain. He will be a laborer together with God. So far as he follows God's directions, he will be successful. He may not accomplish what he desires and expects, but he will accomplish what God designs. When a man accomplishes what God designs he shall accomplish, he has reason to be satisfied with his success.

What a man regards as failure, God often regards as success. As the stars, while rolling onward, sometimes seem to have a retrograde movement, so apparent failure is sometimes real success.

The religious man is in harmony with God and with his government. He knows that he does not live in a fatherless and ungoverned world. He may be in the midst of disorder and evil, yet he knows that all things are under the divine control, and that all things shall work together for good to those who love God.

Religion does not put an end to sickness, care, and trouble; but it enables us so to bear them, that our progress toward perfection is increased. Religion does not destroy death; but it takes away its sting, and makes it an introduction to life eternal.

CHAPTER III.

ENTRANCE ON THE RELIGIOUS LIFE.

IT is optional with a man whether he will be a farmer or not. He may decide not to be a farmer, without violating any principle of wisdom or of rectitude. It is not optional with a man whether he will be a religious man or not. He was made to be a religious man. He was made to do right—always to do right. The will of God is the supreme rule of right. He was made to do the will of God.

Obedience to the will of God as made known by nature and by revelation is the duty of every one. Our moral nature teaches us that we are always to do right. The Bible commands us to be holy as God is holy.

One can, at any time he pleases, enter upon a course of intellectual improvement by exercising his mind in perceiving truth. Can he, at any time he pleases, enter upon a course of religious improvement by exercising his powers in obeying God? One can, of his own will, enter upon a course of intellectual improvement: can he, in like manner, enter upon a course of religious improvement?

Man has by nature all the powers necessary in order to obey God. A knowledge of God's character and law is required: he has capacities for knowing. Love to God is required: he has capacities for loving. As he thus has the powers required for obedience, can he not, at any time he chooses, enter on a course of obedience?

The obedience required is something more than external conformity to the law of God. Doubtless man can, by the exercise of his will, break off from vice and do many things which God requires. But God looks beyond the external act to the motive. The obedience which he requires is an obedience springing from love. Can one who is not a religious man enter, by an act of will, upon this course of loving obedience? Can a man enter upon the religious life, just as he can enter upon the intellectual life?

One with scarcely any desire for mental improvement can, by a resolute course of mental exercise, acquire a love for intellectual pursuits. Can one, in like manner, gradually form habits of loving obedience?

These questions relative to entering on the religious life must be answered in the negative. Though man is a free moral agent, he cannot, by mere force of will, enter upon a course of loving obedience to God. The difficulty is not owing to the lack of the requisite powers, but to a want of disposition to use them.

This want of disposition is owing to the disordered condition of man's nature. Men come into the world with dispositions or tendencies which invariably lead them to sin. Universal experience and observation are in keeping with the teachings of the Bible, that all men are sinners—are alienated from God—have not the love of God in them. He who has no love for God cannot render him a loving service.

This stupendous fact or doctrine of natural depravity meets us when we ask, "How shall we enter on the religious life?" Men have tried to ignore it—have denied it; but the unvarying experience of ages, and the explicit declarations of Scripture, cannot be set aside. The fact of depravity is as patent to the observer, as is the fact of gravitation. One may deny the Scripture account of its origin in the fall of Adam; but he cannot deny the fact that all men have done wrong. The doctrine of depravity is not a doctrine peculiar to the Bible any more than the doctrine of gravitation is peculiar to the Bible. The Bible, so far as it has occasion to treat of man, proceeds on the fact of human depravity; so far as it has occasion to treat of material objects, it proceeds on the fact of gravitation. Men might as well deny the doctrine of gravitation because it is recognized in the Bible, as to deny the doctrine of depravity, because it is recognized in the Bible.

The doctrine of depravity has been misrepresented. Its advocates have sometimes used expressions which have been misunderstood, and have awakened prejudices. The Bible does not assert that men are as wicked as they can be, but that they are alienated from the love of God, and are prone to sin. Those who have used the unfortunate phrase "total depravity," have not meant to assert that men are as bad as they can be, and that there are no degrees in depravity. The most depraved creature on earth may become still more depraved.

The Bible does not assert that men are always governed by selfish motives. It recognizes the fact that they may possess praiseworthy qualities. The young man who came to Jesus manifested qualities which led Jesus to love him, though, owing to avarice, he did not enter upon the religious life. There is nothing in the teaching of the Scriptures requiring us to deny that some men not religious are upright in their dealings with others, kind-hearted and affectionate, possessed of many amiable and even noble qualities. What the Scriptures insist on is that men are, by nature, alienated from God, that they have not the love of God in them, and, therefore, are not subject to his law, "neither indeed can be."

Hence, a change in the condition of the soul is necessary in order to entrance upon a course of loving obedience—to entrance upon the religious life.

This change is compared by Christ to a new birth. "Ye must be born again." The apostle compares it to a new creation, "created anew in Christ Jesus." These forms of expression are figurative, and plainly mean more than a mere determination to change one's course in life—a mere resolution to serve God.

This change is ascribed to the agency of the Holy Spirit. The change is a mysterious one. The process is unknown to consciousness, and, of course, cannot be described. The fact that it has taken place is known from the effects which follow. "The wind bloweth where it listeth, and thou hearest the sound thereof, but canst not tell whence it cometh and whither it goeth. So is every one that is born of the spirit."

A divine power, effecting such a change in the condition of the soul as shall render it capable of entering upon a course of penitent, trusting, loving obedience, is necessary. This is clearly taught in the Bible, and is confirmed by human experience. Multitudes have been convinced of the duty of loving and serving God, and have endeavored to render obedience to his holy law. Their efforts have revealed their guilt and moral weakness. Some have given over striving, and have returned to their sinful courses. Others have thrown themselves on the converting mercy of God.

The Bible recognizes the depraved, sinful condition of men, and provides a method for their recovery to holiness. The religion of the Bible is a religion for fallen men. The Son of Man came to save the lost.

CHAPTER IV.

NOTICE OF SOME ERRORS.

THE change in the condition of the soul, whereby it is rendered capable of entering upon a course of penitent, believing, loving obedience, is sometimes called regeneration, sometimes conversion. When the former term is used, the attention is turned to the cause—the Holy Spirit; when the latter term is used, the attention is turned to the effect—the change in the voluntary actions of the subject.

The relation of conversion to the religious life, is not rightly apprehended by all. We sometimes hear it spoken of as the chief element of the religious life. We hear it said that the great object of effort is the conversion of men. It is regarded as a passport to heaven.

It is difficult to attach undue importance

to conversion. It is difficult to attach undue importance to the beginning of any laudable course of action. Conversion is the beginning of the religious life.

It is not difficult to attach undue importance to certain notions connected with conversion. Because there is such a thing as conversion, it does not follow that all our ideas respecting it are correct.

Some persons have in their minds a formula to which they would have all cases conformed. There must be a process of anxiety and distress, of weeping, reading the Bible, and praying, followed by peace and joy. In their view, he who has passed through these processes, has "experienced religion." A reformed mode of life must follow; but the great work is done. These persons are continually looking back to their conversion. Their hope of salvation is founded on the genuineness of their conversion. The great question with them is: "Was my conversion genuine?"

We are not authorized to form a theory of conversion to which all cases must be conformed under pain of being regarded as spurious. There is a general resemblance in the exercises connected with the beginning of the religious life; there is also great diversity. In some cases the fears are greatly excited; in other cases there is a total absence of fear. In some cases there is a deep sense of guilt—remorse; in other cases, a calm conviction of sin and ruin. In some cases there is a conscious feeling of sin forgiven; in others, a faint hope of mercy. Some persons can point to the place and time when the change took place; others can point only to the changed desires and aspirations of the soul.

These are diversities of exercises, the result of the same Spirit. A man should not ask whether he has been converted according to some prescribed formula; but whether his present feelings, thoughts, and actions show that he is in harmony with God.

The recorded experiences of men of eminent piety are interesting and instructive. They show a great variety in the immediate causes of attention to the subject of religion, and a great variety in the mental exercises preceding and accompanying entrance upon the religious life.

No one should attempt to conform his experience to the example of any one. The Scriptures set forth clearly what we must do to be saved. They do not require us to have an experience after the type of Paul, or of Wesley, or of Edwards. They require us to repent, and to believe on the Lord Jesus Christ.

In the preceding pages, the attempt has been made to give a clear idea of the religious life—to show that religion is not a creed, or a form, or something added to the secular life; but a life of progressive obedience to the will of God.

The attempt has also been made to show why a change usually termed conversion or regeneration is necessary in order to entering on the religious life.

Incorrect views in regard to conversion have been exposed, in order to prepare the way to show how one may enter upon the religious life.

CHAPTER V.

PENITENCE.

WE have seen that the religious life is a life of obedience to the will of God. The will of God has reference to all the actions of life, whether we eat or drink, or whatever we do. In what way can a sinner enter on this life?

It is certain that a sinner will not become a religious man unless he resolves to become one; but will his resolving to become a religious man, make him a religious man? Can he, by an act of will, change the current of his moral life from disobedience to obedience? or can he, by an act of will, enter upon a course of action which will gradually effect this change?

We have seen that he cannot do this. We have seen that his inability is owing not to any deficiency of power so far as voluntary action is concerned, but to want of inclination. It is the inability of the child who cannot render a loving obedience to his father, because he has no love for him. So long as love is entirely wanting, he cannot render a loving obedience.

We have seen that by nature man is alienated from God. This alienation sometimes appears in the form of positive hostility, illustrating the assertion of the Apostle, that "the carnal mind is enmity against God." Of all men it can be said in the words of Jesus: "Ye have not the love of God in you." Where there is this alienation, there can be no loving obedience. Hence, as we have seen, there is need of a change in the condition of the soul—a change effected by divine power.

When a sinner asks, "What must I do to be saved?" the divine answer is not, "Enter on a course of obedience which will gradually become more and more perfect;" nor is it, "Wait inactive till the Spirit has produced a change in the condition of your soul." The Divine answer is: "Repent, and believe on the Lord Jesus Christ."

The first thing to be done by him who would become a Christian is *to repent*. Hence, he needs to know why he should repent, what it is to repent, and what is the relation which repentance has to the religious life.

Because a man cannot convert himself, it does not follow that he cannot do anything toward his conversion. A certain amount of knowledge is necessary to his conversion. That knowledge he can acquire.

The sinner should repent because he is a sinner. He has done nothing but sin since he became capable of moral action. He was made to do right—to do right at all times and under all circumstances. He has, in many instances, done wrong when the claims of right were clearly set before him. He has done many things without considering whether they were right or wrong. He was made to render a loving obedience to the will of God. He has not loved God, and has not performed a single act of obedience; that is, of obedience prompted by love. He is under obligation to be holy, but he is unholy—every act of his life is unholy—by positive transgression or defect in motive.

He may not be an immoral man. He may be a moral, amiable, affectionate man; but he has lived without God. All his acts are tainted with rebellion against his lawful sovereign. He is a sinner, and hence it is reasonable that he should repent.

What is it to repent? What is repentance? Anxiety, fear, in view of the consequences of sin, is not repentance. The sinner has abundant reasons for fear. God has said, "The soul that sinneth, it shall die." Justice and judgment are the habitation of His throne. He has declared that He will by no means clear the guilty. The consequences of sin are set forth in language the most appalling. It is reasonable that the sinner should fear the wine-press of the wrath of Almighty God. But fear, terror, is not repentance.

The uneasiness, self-disapprobation, the remorse which follows the commission of sin, is not repentance. Remorse is deep distress; but remorse is not repentance. Hence, efforts to increase the excitement of fear, or the intensity of remorse, by listening to alarming exhortations, or reading books appealing to the fears, or by visiting scenes of excitement, furnish no aids to repentance. Such efforts imply ignorance of the true nature of repentance.

It is true that fear and remorse may have some connection with repentance. A sense of danger may lead one to take measures for safety. A sense of guilt, remorse, may awaken the desire of deliverance, may lead to proper efforts for that end.

A not uncommon error in regard to repentance is, that it consists in feelings of distress; and that, the greater the distress, the more thorough the repentance. So far is this from being true, that there may be intense distress in view of sin, without the slightest feeling of penitence. Penitence consists, for the most part, in feeling—in sorrowful feeling; but all sorrowful feeling is not penitence.

A child, in a moment of forgetfulness or passion, has disobeyed and grieved his loving parent. The child is sorry for his conduct. He may not have any fear of punishment; he may feel sure of prompt forgiveness: but he cannot forgive himself. His sorrow, not his fear of punishment, leads him to resolve that he will never repeat the act of disobedience. He is penitent: he has repented of his disobedience.

When one feels sorry that he has sinned against a loving and holy God; when he is sorry for sin for its own sake, irrespective of consequences; when his sorrow leads him earnestly to desire that he may sin no more;

when he feels that he has forfeited the favor of God, and that his condemnation is just; when he feels that it is an evil and bitter thing to sin against God; he is penitent.

He is now in a proper condition to receive pardon, if provision has been made for the exercise of the pardoning power. Penitence does not atone for sin. Sorrow for having transgressed the law does not sever the connection between the transgression and the penalty.

Penitence is the appropriate condition for the reception of pardon. No executive would pardon a criminal whose only feeling with respect to his crime was a fear of punishment, and who cherished the same disposition which led to the commission of the crime. True penitence does not merit pardon, but is the appropriate and necessary condition of pardon.

Penitence is the antecedent of faith. The sinner is commanded to repent, and to believe the gospel. What is the penitent to believe? He is to believe that God, for Christ's sake, will forgive his sins, and grant him the aids of divine grace. Why should he believe this? Because God has promised it. There can be no better reason for believing a thing than the fact that God has uttered it—the fact that it rests on the veracity of God.

This promise is made to the penitent only. Hence, none but the penitent can believe. Penitence is thus the necessary condition of faith.

CHAPTER VI.

HOW TO REPENT.

How shall a man repent? Can he, by an act of will, bring his mind into the condition termed penitence? This question must be answered in the negative; but it does not follow that a man cannot do anything relating to repentance. There are essential conditions within his power. No man can reasonably refuse to do that which is within his power, because there are some things beyond his power.

In order to repentance, a man must be convinced that he is a sinner; not that he has committed some sins, but that the whole course of his life has been a sinful course. To this end, a knowledge of God's law is necessary. The sinner must know what God requires of him, and must compare his conduct with God's requirements. He who is ignorant of God's law, or, knowing it, does not compare his conduct with it, cannot be convinced of sin. He may feel uncomfortable; but he cannot feel that he is a sinner. It is not affirmed that the study of God's law and of one's conduct will produce true conviction of sin; but that this knowledge and comparison are essential conditions of conviction. Let no one who neglects these conditions of repentance say, "I cannot repent." These conditions are clearly within his power. The special aid of the Holy Spirit is not necessary in order that one may learn the truths necessary to repentance. The sinner must have a knowledge of the character of God. He may have a knowledge of the divine law, and may know that he has been guilty of disobedience; the feeling consequent upon that knowledge will be greatly modified by his view of the character of the Lawgiver and Judge. One may see that he has disobeyed the stern commands of a just Ruler. One may see that he has disobeyed the loving commands of a Father who is most anxious for his welfare, and whose commands have reference to his highest good, and who has mingled entreaties with his commands. The feelings of the latter, in view of his disobedience, must differ widely from those of the former.

In order to penitence, the sinner must know the character of the Being whose laws he has transgressed. He needs to know the character of God.

The character of God is clearly revealed in his Holy Word. Hence, he who would repent must study the Bible, that he may become acquainted with the character of God. "Acquaint thyself with God, and be at peace with him." There can be no peace with God for a sinner, except through penitence and pardon.

The sinner, therefore, should study the Bible; not because it is a meritorious act lessening his guilt, but that he may have the knowledge of God necessary to repentance. He who looks upon God as a hard Master, cannot have toward him the feelings of a true penitent.

Men who have not studied the Bible have, commonly, very defective views of the Divine character. It is true that no one can, by searching, find out God to perfection. The finite cannot fully comprehend the infinite. Still, man can learn that which is clearly revealed.

The sinner can learn from the Bible that God is just; that he must be just at all times. He can also learn that God is benevolent; that his benevolence prompted the sublimest act which the universe has witnessed. "God so loved the world that he gave his only begotten Son, that whosoever believeth in him should not perish, but have everlasting life." He can learn that God is not willing that any man should perish; but desires that all should come to repentance. He learns that "Like as a father pitieth his children, so the Lord pitieth them that fear him;" that as the father ran to receive the returning prodigal, the Lord is ready to receive and love and save every repentant sinner.

One says, "I have studied the law of God, and I know that its requirements are just and wise, and adapted to promote the happiness of man. I have learned something of God. I have learned that he is a holy, just, loving, merciful Being. I know that I have failed to render obedience to the law, and to feel toward God as I ought. I know that I have done nothing but sin, either by transgression or defect. Still, I have not the feelings which constitute penitence, and I know not how to awaken them. I know how I ought to feel; but how to get the feeling, I know not."

There is evidently need of a power from without—an influence to cause the truths perceived to make on the mind the impression they are adapted to make. There is need of the influence of the Holy Spirit. How shall that influence be secured?

Christ says, "If ye, being evil, know how to give good gifts unto your children, how much more shall your Heavenly Father give the Holy Spirit to them that ask him?" The implied promise is to those who ask him—to those who ask, feeling their need. There is a theory that God will hear the prayers of converted persons, and of converted persons only. There is no warrant for this theory in the word of God. Let the sinner take God at his word; let him ask for that which is essential to his repentance—the influence of the Holy Spirit.

CHAPTER VII.

THE TRUE IDEA OF FAITH.

THE conditions of salvation are repentance and faith. Through the exercise of these, the sinner enters upon the religious life.

We have endeavored to set forth the true idea of repentance. What is the true idea of faith? What is it to believe on the Lord Jesus Christ? What is that faith which justifies?

Faith is something more than the mental act of believing. Every one knows what it is to believe a proposition. Faith includes the act of believing; but it is something more. You believe that Jesus Christ died for sinners. That is not believing on Christ. You believe that he spoke the truth when he said, "Him that cometh to me, I will in no wise cast out." That is not believing on

Christ. You believe that God exists. That is not having "faith in God." You believe that God has promised forgiveness for Christ's sake, to the penitent sinner. You have not the slightest doubt of the fact. That is not having faith in Christ.

Faith is confidence in a personal being. Faith in Christ is confidence—trust in his promises and his character. One may believe that he is trustworthy without trusting in him. Belief may be general. Faith must be particular. One has faith in Christ when he trusts him as his personal Saviour.

Like many of the simplest operations of the human mind, faith is often spoken of in a manner adapted to mislead the hearer. It is spoken of as the instrument of salvation—as something which is antagonistic to, or takes the place of, works in the method of salvation. The frequent personification of faith has a tendency to mislead—to turn the mind away from the simple, indefinable idea of trust.

The idea of faith, of confidence in a person, of trust, is familiar to all men. It forms a part of their every-day experience. Religious faith is simply the realization of this idea in the religious life.

A father who has never deceived his child, promises him a book on the morrow. The child has perfect confidence in his father's promise. He feels sure that he shall have his book at the appointed time. He trusts his father—has faith in his father.

This state of mind is strictly analogous to that which constitutes faith in Christ.

Perhaps the child has contracted a debt at a bookstore. He asks his father for money to pay the debt. The father says, "I will pay it for you." The son believes him—trusts him to pay the debt. Soon afterward the father says, "I have paid that debt." The child believes him, and has no further anxiety about it.

Christ says that he will forgive and save every penitent sinner. The sinner who believes him—trusts him—exercises faith. His sins are forgiven, and he is placed in a condition to render a loving obedience to the will of God. A right spirit is renewed within him, whereby he can enter upon a course of obedience which shall be "as the shining light which shineth more and more unto the perfect day."

It may be said that belief and trust are not voluntary. One cannot believe a proposition by willing to believe it. One cannot trust by willing to trust. How, then, can he exercise faith?

It is not affirmed that the state of mind termed confidence, trust, faith, can be the direct result of an act of will. The necessary conditions of faith are within one's power. Just as one can examine the evidence adapted to produce belief, one can examine the evidence adapted to produce faith. In order to believe, the mind must have adequate evidence of the truth of a proposition. In order to trust, the mind must have adequate evidence of the trustworthiness of the object of trust.

Will an examination of the trustworthiness of Christ produce trust—faith? If, as will be the case, the evidence of trustworthiness is found to be overwhelming, will faith follow, just as belief follows the evidence of truth?

There are many persons who have no doubt whatever as to Christ's trustworthiness, and of his ability and willingness to save, who do not trust in him, and who say they cannot trust in him.

They desire salvation, they have sorrow for their sins—perhaps they are truly penitent; but they cannot believe that Christ will forgive and save them. They cannot say or feel, "I am forgiven and saved; for Christ has promised to forgive and save me." They cannot trust him for pardon and the spirit of obedience.

Why cannot they trust the most trustworthy being in the universe?

The Scriptures speak of an evil heart of unbelief. Reference is had to the natural alienation of the soul from God. Owing to this departure from the living God, the influence of the Holy Spirit is necessary to the exercise of repentance and faith. In a most important sense, repentance and faith are gifts of God : at the same time, they are the sinner's own act.

The mental processes which precede the conscious exercise of faith, differ in different persons. Some, convinced of their sin and ruin, seeing the method of pardon, accept it with joy, having no experience of difficulties in the way of so doing. All such persons ascribe their repentance and faith to the influence of the Holy Spirit. They are all prepared to say with Paul, " By the grace of God I am what I am."

Others find many difficulties in the way. They see what they ought to do, but are unable to do it. After many fruitless efforts, finding their condition to be no better, but growing worse, they are driven to despair of all efforts, and to cry out with sinking Peter, " Save, Lord, or I perish ! " Driven to despair of themselves, they are shut up to the necessity of throwing themselves on the mercy of Christ—of trusting in Christ.

If a man is fully convinced that he is a sinner—a lost sinner—and that he cannot save himself ; if he has a desire to be saved from sin as well as from the consequences of sin ; if he sees that the will of God is a most reasonable and desirable directory of life; if he seeks to conform his whole life to that will, looking to God for help, and relying upon the merits of Christ as the ground of his acceptance with God, he has a right to regard himself as a converted man. No depths of sorrow and no heights of joy can furnish evidence so satisfactory. He need not trouble himself because he cannot adopt the language used by others in giving expression to their experience.

CHAPTER VIII.

THE RELIGIOUS LIFE PROGRESSIVE.

CONVERSION is the beginning of the religious life—of a life of obedience to the will of God. It places the soul in a condition rendering the formation of holy habits possible. Religious habits are formed just as other habits are formed. Habits of obedience are formed by the repetition of acts of obedience; habits of self-denial are formed by the repetition of acts of self-denial; habits of prayer are formed by the repetition of acts of prayer.

The gospel is a scheme for the restoration of the image of God to the soul of man. This scheme does not make provision for a sudden restoration of the divine image. No doubt the Holy Spirit can make a sinner perfectly holy in an instant of time; but the dispensation of the Spirit is not after that manner. A capacity for genuine obedience is given to the soul once dead in trespasses and sins. A germ of holiness is implanted. Then appears, first the blade, then the ear, after that the full corn in the ear. The religious life is a life of advancement in holiness. Means and aids are furnished so that the soul can go from strength to strength, till it becomes holy as God is holy. The object of redemption, the restoration of the soul to holiness, is then accomplished.

The character of one's religious life will depend very much on the course pursued at the outset. All men admit the importance of right instruction as to conversion. The truths necessary to conversion must be carefully taught. Some persons who insist on this, seem in a measure indifferent to instructions subsequent to conversion. They assume that the converted man will be saved. They seem to think that the chief matter is disposed of, and that the remaining portion of the religious life is of little consequence.

Let it be remembered that conversion is the beginning of the religious life. It is important that one should begin right. It is equally important that he should go on right.

The young convert is often told that he must work for God—that, having been converted himself, he must labor for the conversion of others. He is told that he must go and work in the Lord's vineyard. He is thus led to believe that his chief duties as a religious man consist in exhorting sinners, attending and taking part in meetings, and in public efforts for promoting the interests of the church. He gives himself zealously to these objects, to the neglect of the every-day duties of life. He may be conscious of this neglect, but decides that, in the supposed conflict of duties, those in which he is engaged claim precedence.

Now, he who has been rightly instructed, knows that in the divine government there are no "conflicts of laws"—no conflicts of duties. It is true that every converted man is to work in God's vineyard. With Paul, he should ask, "Lord, what wilt thou have me to do?" He should seek to do at all times what God would have him to do. He will be led to see that he may be working for God as truly when he is guiding the plough as when he is leading the social worship of God. He will learn that zeal in the performance of one class of duties will not atone for the neglect of another class of duties. He will see that he has but one thing to do—the will of God; and that all the requirements of that will are equally imperative.

When one sets out on his religious life, a correct knowledge of his duty is of the utmost importance. It is owing to the want of this knowledge that there are so few, comparatively, who illustrate the progressive character of the Christian life. Many Christians seem to be stationary. They have been converted; a great change has taken place; they are better men than they were before; but there is no visible increase in goodness. At the end of the year, or of a term of years, they are no more Christ-like than they were when first converted.

Men are converted that they may become like Christ; that they may grow in grace—make progress in holiness.

To acquire the requisite knowledge, recourse should be had to the study of the Bible. The Bible is the guide-book of the religious man. It should be studied with prayer for the illuminating influences of the Holy Spirit. We need to know the mind of the Spirit; and the aid of the Spirit is necessary for the attainment of that knowledge.

Some persons read the Bible as a religious duty, without any further definite aim. The Bible was given us to teach us what to do.

CHAPTER IX.

JUSTICE AND MERCY.

PRAYER is one of the first acts of the converted soul. When Ananias was sent to Paul, it was told him, "Behold, he prayeth." Ananias recognized prayer as the act of a converted soul; he addressed Saul by the title of "Brother."

The truths connected with the right exercise of prayer should be clearly apprehended. When a man prays, he asks an undeserved favor from God. He has sinned, and has forfeited all claim to the divine favor. He can come to God as a suppliant, and only as a suppliant. He has no occasion to ask for justice at the hand of God. To receive justice were to receive utter ruin. What man needs is mercy.

Prayer is founded on the fact that God is merciful. He is also just; and justice requires the strict enforcement of law. Justice and judgment are the habitation of his throne. Mercy and truth go before him. His mercy endureth forever; yet he will by no means spare the guilty. He is not willing that any should perish; yet he declares, "The soul that sinneth, it shall die." We find here apparently conflicting utterances in regard to the character of the High and Holy One.

God is a perfect Being. There can be no inconsistencies in his holy character. If he is just, he can show mercy only in consistency with justice.

The claims of justice are supreme. Whenever a just action is set before us, we instinctively perceive that it ought to be done. Let a course be set before us, adapted to gratify our desires, but involving injustice toward others, and we see at once that it ought not to be taken. The human mind recognizes justice as the supreme law. Justice is the fundamental law of the state; it is higher than the constitution. It is the grand constitutional law of the Universe, to which every act of the divine government is conformed.

The question arises, "How can God show mercy? How can he remit the penalty of the just law, and still be just?" Unless we have a clear idea of the relations of justice and mercy in the divine economy, we are not prepared to ask for mercy without danger of asking amiss. The Apostle informs us that one reason for our not receiving is our asking amiss.

A vague idea that God is merciful does not authorize a request for mercy. We are authorized to ask for such things as it is consistent for God to give. One would shrink with horror from the idea of asking God to make a false statement for his benefit. But this request would not be more irreverent than asking him to do an act of injustice for your benefit. For God to show mercy without regard to justice is as impossible for him as it is to lie. The impossibility in both cases is the result of the perfection of his nature.

Notwithstanding the clear teachings of the Scriptures as to the justice of God, many persons have inadequate views on the subject. They think that the exercise of justice is optional with God; that he can, if he pleases, overlook the violations of his law, just as the parent can overlook the transgressions of parental rules. They do not see that the law is not the arbitrary expression of his will, but the transcript of his holy character. The law is as it is, because God is as he is. It cannot be different from what it is, because God cannot be different from what he is. Hence he must be just; and, if merciful, must be merciful in consistency with justice.

Justice relates to everything pertaining to the divine government. Mercy relates to guilty persons. Mercy is favor shown to the guilty—the undeserving. God must be just.

He may be merciful. He cannot be merciful at the expense of justice. Hence, there must be a way whereby he can be just, and yet justify the ungodly. To justify the ungodly is to remit the penalty of their disobedience, and to treat them as if they were righteous—to confer on them the rewards of obedience.

God has declared that he has provided a way for the exercise of mercy. The gospel, the good news of God, is a revelation of that way. The incarnation, obedience, sufferings, and death of Christ, are the prominent facts of the method of reconciling justice and mercy in the government of God. "God so loved the world that he gave his only begotten Son, that whosoever believeth in him should not perish, but have everlasting life." Christ "loved us and gave himself for us;" "he was obedient unto death, even the death of the cross;" he "bare our sins in his own body on the tree;" was "made for us righteousness and sanctification and redemption." These, and many similar passages, clearly show that God, for Christ's sake, in view of his obedience and death, forgives penitent sinners, and counts them as righteous, and gives them the aid of the Holy Spirit, whereby they may enter upon a life of progressive holiness, and finally fully recover the lost image of God.

This is God's explanation of his method of mercy toward sinful men. If we are willing to receive it on God's authority, and to receive it just as he has given it, it is a simple method. The facts which are the grounds of the sinner's pardon are clearly stated, and pardon is freely offered. It is man's business to receive them on the authority of God, and to act in view of them by exercising repentance toward God and faith toward our Lord Jesus Christ.

God gives his instructions and commands. Men ought to receive those instructions and obey those commands. Many men are not disposed so to do. Like Nicodemus, they are disposed to ask, "How can these things be?" They desire to understand the philosophy of God's method of salvation, before they avail themselves of it. In so doing, they are as unwise as one would be, who, having received a telegram informing him how to act in order to save his life, should delay action until the laws of electricity, and their application to the construction of the telegraph were explained to him. Immediate action would save him; delay from whatever cause would effect his ruin.

CHAPTER X.

PRAYER.

In view of the relation of justice to mercy, it is plain that the sinner must approach God in prayer in the name of Christ; that is, he must confess his utter unworthiness, and ask for Christ's sake, for those things which God permits him to ask for.

What are we permitted to ask for? We are permitted to ask for those things which we need for our temporal and spiritual well-being. "Be careful for nothing," that is, do not be anxious and troubled, "but in everything, by prayer and supplication with thanksgiving, make known your requests unto God." The field of petition is thus exceeding broad. The promises are very explicit. "Ask, and it shall be given you: seek, and ye shall find. For every one that asketh receiveth."

Much that is called prayer is tentatory, experimental. One asks for many things, not because he expects to receive them, but because it is customary to ask for them. He has an idea that by asking for a great many things he may get something; or that some good may result from his prayers. Eliminate from the records of prayer all prayers of this description, and the sum total will be greatly diminished!

It would not be decorous to ask a friend for a variety of things with no expectation of receiving them. What shall be said of similar conduct with respect to God?

God's promises in relation to the answer of prayer are conditioned on our asking in a proper manner for things in accordance with His will. We ask amiss when we do not ask with a submissive spirit. However much we may desire an object, we ought not to desire it in opposition to the will of God. The expression of a desire in opposition to the will of God, is something very different from prayer. The renewed soul desires to be in harmony with God. He does not wish to have his own way, when that way is disapproved of God.

God knows the end from the beginning. He knows whether the granting of our petition would be for our own good, and the best interests of His kingdom. Every prayer should therefore be offered with the implied condition that it be in accordance with the will of God. Some seem to think that an intensity of desire which will take no denial, is the highest form of earnest prayer. The most earnest and affecting prayer ever offered, closed with the words: "Not my will, but Thine be done."

We are to ask in faith. To ask in faith is to ask with confidence that God will do what he has promised to do. Faith, we have seen, is confidence in God. To pray in faith is to pray with confidence in God.

Some persons think that in order to pray

in faith, we must believe that the specific petition will be granted—that it will be granted if we believe that it will be granted. We purpose to pray for the conversion of a person. In order to pray in faith, it is thought that we must believe, without a doubt, that he will be converted. If he is not converted, it will be owing to our want of faith—to our want of believing that he will be converted.

Those who entertain this view, may make great efforts to believe, but without success. Belief does not follow an act of the will. We cannot believe without evidence, any more than the eye can see without light. We cannot believe that a person will be converted unless we have evidence that he will be converted. Unless God has revealed His purpose to convert him for whom we pray, we have no adequate evidence that he will be converted; hence, we cannot believe that he will be converted. We may, for various reasons, think it probable that he will be converted; but this state is far from that belief amounting to certainty which some men regard as the necessary condition of praying in faith.

This erroneous view in regard to the prayer of faith, results from not distinguishing between the faith for the performance of miracles, and the faith connected with the daily life of the Christian. Miraculous faith was given with miraculous power, if it did not constitute that power.

It is not desirable that God should give us whatever we ask for. It is far better that he should be guided by his own infinite wisdom, than by our desires. If his promises were unconditional, we should have the power of omnipotence without infinite wisdom to direct it. As it is, we have both the power and the wisdom of God for our portion.

We must pray with a forgiving spirit. "Forgive us our debts, as we forgive our debtors." We are here authorized to pray for forgiveness as we forgive. In using this formula, we may ask God not to forgive us.

"If ye forgive not men their trespasses, neither will your Heavenly Father forgive you." The language is very explicit; the condition is unqualified. The Christian spirit is evidently a forgiving spirit.

The absence of hatred toward those who have injured us is not forgiveness. The hatred may be quiescent, but it may be in the heart. When one's attention is turned wholly away from his enemies, he is not conscious of enmity toward them. He may pray, and think that he has met the conditions of successful prayer, but he has not. He must, "from his heart," forgive. When we think of the unkind criticisms, the envy and ill-concealed dislike which are too often witnessed among professing Christians, it would seem that we must make another large deduction from the amount of genuine prayer.

CHAPTER XI.

INFLUENCE OF THE SPIRIT.

WE have seen that the change in the soul, rendering it capable of entering upon the religious life, is wrought by the Holy Spirit. We are taught by the Scriptures that the influence of the Spirit is necessary to the progress of that life. God has promised that influence to those who ask him; that is, to those who ask from right motives—in the right way.

This influence is needed to give clear perceptions of truth and duty. The influence of the Spirit upon the mind, in connection with a knowledge of the truth, is frequently spoken of in the Bible. Christ says, "He shall guide you into all truth." "He shall teach you all things, and bring all things to your remembrance, whatsoever I have said unto you."

Every reader of the Bible has been struck with the place it assigns to truth. It everywhere insists on the importance of a knowledge of the truth.

The reason of this is obvious. Man was made to act wisely—rightly. All wise and right action is put forth under the guidance of truth. A knowledge of truth is the necessary condition of wise action. A man cannot act wisely under the leading of error. Error cannot be a directory of wise action. The Bible requires not merely a belief of the truth, but actions in accordance with the truth. A true creed is not merely to be believed; it is to be lived. An orthodox creed is the condition of an orthodox life. If it does not produce an orthodox life, the reception of it, as a belief, will be of no benefit.

The study of the Bible should be accompanied with prayer for the illuminating and quickening influences of the Holy Spirit, that we may have an accurate knowledge of the truth, and be led to act in accordance with it.

The influence of the Spirit is needed in our efforts to pray. As prayer is the offering of our desires to God, only pure and holy desires should be offered. Our desires need the purifying influences of the Spirit. There is a preparation of the heart for prayer which can be complete only by the aid of the Spirit. "The Spirit also helpeth our infirmities: for we know not what we should pray for as we ought."

Prayer is the act of a sinner—a converted sinner—speaking to the High and Holy One, who inhabiteth eternity. It should not be a formal, thoughtless act. In every approach to God, the aid of the Holy Spirit should be earnestly sought.

The Scriptures speak of a very intimate relation between the Spirit and the followers of Christ. He is said to dwell within believers. Paul speaks of "His Spirit which dwelleth in you," and of "the Holy Ghost which dwelleth in us." "Know ye not that ye are the temple of God, and that the Spirit of God dwelleth in you?"

Without attempting to describe this mysterious indwelling, we are certain that it indicates a very intimate connection between the Spirit of God and the mind of the converted sinner. It implies the communion of the Spirit spoken of in the apostolic benediction. Such a presence must influence the entire condition of the soul and all its exercises, causing them to become more and more conformed to the divine will—sanctifying them, setting them apart, devoting them more perfectly to God's service. Men are thus sanctified by the Spirit.

This indwelling is not a forced indwelling. It is conditioned on the conduct of the subject. We are told to "grieve not the Holy Spirit;" and the Psalmist prays, "Take not Thy Holy Spirit from me." It is thus plainly intimated that the Spirit will not dwell with uncongenial souls. He cannot abide where there is envy, wrath, hatred, or cherished sin in any form. We are sometimes restrained from sin by a view of the consequence. Regard for the opinions and feelings of our brethren sometimes acts as a restraint. We do not wish to lose their respect and confidence. There is no consequence so disastrous as the withdrawal of the Holy Spirit. Our prayers for His presence should be most earnest, and our conduct such as shall cause Him to abide with us. If our bodies are temples of the Holy Ghost, they should not be put to uses inconsistent with the presence of the august Indweller.

The Spirit is called by Christ, the Comforter. In this world of sin and sorrow we often need a comforter. In the Spirit we have a Comforter who knows our most secret sorrows, and who can, without the aid of words, minister comfort and consolation; or who can take the words of inspiration, and show how exactly they are fitted to our case.

It is to be feared that the relation of the Spirit to the religious life is not so clearly understood as it should be.

CHAPTER XII.

MEDITATION.—SECRET PRAYER.

HASTE is characteristic of the age. Much is done in a superficial manner because it is done in haste. Thought, care, time, are necessary to thoroughness. The spirit of the age has its influence on the religious life. Against this influence we should carefully guard. God's work should be thoroughly done. We have only God's work to do.

The Christian ought to be active. He is told, "Whatsoever thy hand findeth to do, do it with thy might." There is much to be done in the way of promoting the cause of Christ. The Christian may be led by good motives to undertake more than he can properly perform. It is not enough that he is prompted by genuine zeal. His zeal must be regulated—directed by the will of God.

The zealous performance of one duty will not atone for the neglect of another duty. Efforts for the conversion of men will not atone for the neglect of those duties which are essential to the soul's highest progress in holiness.

It has been said that the piety of a former age was more deep and spiritual than that of the present age; because, owing to less urgent calls for Christian activity, men gave more attention to the interests of their own souls. We are far from saying that the former days were better than the present. It is not certain that the piety of those days was superior to that of the present. While it may be admitted that more cultivation was bestowed on some traits of Christian character, others were sadly neglected. The most spiritually-minded man in those days saw no sin in the traffic and general use of ardent spirits, or in slavery and the slave-trade. John Newton abandoned the slave-trade, not because he regarded it as sinful, but because he desired a more humane method of gaining a livelihood. This was after he was converted, but before he became a preacher.

It must be admitted that Christians of the present day have clearer and more comprehensive views of duty than Christians of former times had. Hence the various forms of activity put forth for the furtherance of Christ's kingdom. It is not affirmed that these are always wisely planned, or that they are pursued by all with right motives. But leaving out all that is defective, there is more to rejoice over than at any former period of Christian history. This activity may lead to the neglect of duties equally important, but less prominent in the view of men. The study of divine truth, meditation, and secret prayer, are essential to the soul's progress in holiness—the great end of the religious life.

The truth of God, contained in his word, must be brought into contact with the mind, that, by the power of the Spirit, it may exert a transforming influence on the character. Christ says that the instrument used by the Spirit in the work of sanctification, is the truth. "Sanctify them through thy truth: Thy word is truth." The truth, therefore, is not only a directory of duty, but the instrument of a divine influence by which the soul is made more holy. Hence the importance of meditation—of keeping the truth before the mind.

That a truth may make an impression on the mind, it must be made the subject of continued and exclusive attention. It is thus that the beautiful thoughts of our best poets are appreciated, and the teachings of our best philosophers fully understood. Apart from the mysterious influence of the Spirit, frequent meditation on portions of the divine Word must bring us into closer sympathy with God and into greater conformity to his will. When the sanctifying influence of the Spirit is taken into view, the duty of meditation appears still more important. Its faithful performance will greatly increase our efficiency in our efforts for the promotion of Christ's kingdom.

Every Christian knows the importance of secret prayer. The example of Christ, and his direct precepts, require the earnest performance of this duty. He who neglects it feels that he enters upon his daily work without the preparation needed to keep him steadfast to duty. Departures from God begin, for the most part, by a neglect of secret prayer.

CHAPTER XIII.

DOING GOOD.

CHRISTIANS are said to be laborers together with God. They are to follow the example of Him who went about doing good. Doing good was the business of Christ, and should be the business of his followers.

"How can doing good be the business of my life, when I am obliged to toil for my daily bread? I must be excused from labors to do good," says the laborer.

"My business demands all my care and energies," says the merchant. "I have no time for anything else. I can give money: but I must be excused from personal labors to do good."

"I have been called to occupy an important position," says the judge. "My labors are exhausting. The little leisure I have must be given to rest, or I shall lose my health. I must be excused from labors to do good."

Shall these men be excused from labors to do good? Are these pleas valid?

With respect to many forms of doing good, they are valid. The laborer cannot be called upon to spend a large portion of his time in visiting the poor, or in giving instruction to the young. The merchant cannot be called upon to conduct a prayer-meeting at an hour when he must meet his customers, or not meet them at all. The judge cannot be called upon to attend a protracted meeting when his court is in session. There are many ways of doing good which are not required of these men. It is required of them that they should do whatever they do to the glory of God.

Because some forms of doing good are not required of a man, it does not follow that he is excused from efforts to do good. Every one is required to do good as he has opportunity; and every one should be watchful for opportunities of doing good.

Every man is bound to spend his whole life in doing good. What he is to do will be determined by the circumstances in which he is placed. He is to ask God daily, "Lord, what wilt Thou have me to do?" and when he does what God requires of him, he does good in the most efficient way. The first duty of every one is to do good in his ordinary calling. The laborer can do good in his daily work. Let him do everything he does heartily, as unto God; let him be faithful in all his work; let him be faithful in all things; let him be kind and considerate of the feelings of others; let him show, by a consistent life, his regard for the authority of God; and, by his temper, that he has been with Jesus: and he will do good every day of his life. His influence for good may be much greater than that of many who are prominent in works of benevolence.

The merchant can do good in his daily calling. If he is diligent in business because it is God's will that he should be diligent; if his uprightness secures the confidence of all who know him; if his statements are implicitly relied on; if men see that he always obeys the golden rule, they will credit his profession of Christianity. He will be a daily witness for Christ, though he may never speak of his personal experience in matters of religion. Thus, men in every department of life may serve God in their calling.

In addition to the faithful discharge of the duties of their calling, men should do good as they have opportunity. They can do good by speaking a word of encouragement to the weary, a word of sympathy to the sad and suffering, a word of counsel to the perplexed or tempted, and by giving, according to their ability, to those in want.

In these, and in many other ways, men can do good outside of the duties of their daily calling.

Men influence by what they are, as well as by what they say and do. This unconscious influence is sometimes very strong. It may emanate from one by no means remarkable for mental power. Efforts to bring our souls into closer union with God, to become more Christ-like, are, indirectly, efforts to do good. A man's influence for good is proportioned to his likeness to Christ.

CHAPTER XIV.

JUSTICE.—SYMPATHY.—SELF-DENIAL. CROSS-BEARING.

IN mentioning what is required of us, the inspired prophet places justice first. "And what doth the Lord require of thee but to do justly and to love mercy, and to walk humbly with thy God?"

Justice is often thought of as a commonplace duty—as a duty pertaining to morality rather than to religion. In a former chapter, attention has been called to the place occupied by justice in the government of God. As it occupies the first place there, it must occupy the first place as a rule of life.

Let no one imagine that, in a remedial system, justice is less imperative in its claims than under a legal system. Let no one allow his ideas of faith and grace to detract in the least from the supreme claims of justice as a rule of life.

The Christian should be as careful to conform to the rules of justice as if his salvation depended upon it. In all his business transactions, he should be scrupulously just. In all his judgments respecting his fellow men, he should judge righteous judgment. In all his utterances with respect to others, he should have regard to justice.

The object of redemption and the religious life is the restoration of the lost image of God. In order to be like God, one must be just.

But justice is not the only law of life. We are to sympathize with our fellow men. We are to rejoice with them that rejoice, and weep with them that weep.

As sorrow predominates in this world, when we speak of sympathy our thoughts are turned at once to scenes of suffering. The Christian should form habits of sympathy. Sympathy is intended to lead to the assistance of the suffering. When its promptings are judiciously followed, a lovely Christ-like trait of character is developed. He whose sympathies are quick, and who does not allow himself to be misled by them, is esteemed and admired. He is one whose work is to follow Christ in comforting those who mourn, and in binding up the brokenhearted. Habits of sympathy are formed by wise action under the promptings of sympathy.

Right action from sympathy is benevolent action. Benevolent action has for its object the happiness of others. Christian benevolence should have respect both to the temporal and the spiritual good of men. Christ healed the sick, and fed the hungry, and preached the gospel to the poor. We should imitate Him by striving to do good to both the bodies and souls of men. We should not allow the charge to be made that in our regard for the future happiness of men, we are indifferent to their temporal comforts.

It may often be necessary to practice self-denial, in order to provide the means of doing good to others. A man is in want, and we can relieve him by doing without some convenience or luxury. Christian benevolence requires us to practice that self-denial.

Self-denial has not a pleasant aspect to the view of selfishness; but experience teaches that, like all other duties, its performance is pleasant. There is great enjoyment in self-denial for Christ's sake.

A more difficult kind of self-denial is that relating to our desires and passions. Some of the desires of our fallen nature are not eradicated by conversion. Men are not made perfect at their entrance on the religious life. The war within, occasioned by our sinful propensities and desires, is often fierce and long continued. Paul speaks of the law of his members warring against the law of his mind.

The demands of sinful appetites and sinful desires must be denied. The war in the soul must be a fearful war; but victory will be given to him who resolutely, by the grace of God, denies ungodly and worldly lusts.

Taking up the cross is a duty mentioned in connection with self-denial. "Whosoever will come after Me, let him deny himself, and take up his cross, and follow Me." Self-denial and cross-bearing are not generically different. A man denies himself when he refuses indulgence to some desire. He takes up his cross who performs a difficult and painful duty—a duty made difficult and painful by influences from without. A man belonging to an irreligious family becomes a Christian. His avowal of the fact will bring upon him the scorn and dislike of the family. He makes the avowal, thus taking up and bearing his cross. Every Christian should carefully perform duty, however painful, rejoicing that he is counted worthy to suffer for Christ's sake.

Some persons make crosses for themselves,

and think there is merit in bearing them. We should bear the burdens which God imposes; but we should not load ourselves with unnecessary burdens.

CHAPTER XV.

RELIGIOUS CONVERSATION.—SOCIAL WORSHIP.

It is said that those who feared the Lord "spake often one to another." It is natural for persons to converse on themes in which they feel an absorbing interest. The themes connected with salvation and eternal life appeal to man's interest more powerfully than any other themes. They ought to be the most interesting themes that can engage the attention of men. Hence, we should expect that men, especially Christian men, would often make them the subject of conversation. If it is true that out of the abundance of the heart the mouth speaketh, what inference is to be drawn from the fact that we seldom hear persons conversing with interest on matters pertaining to the religious life? Must not we infer that men are more interested in other matters? If so, are they seeking first the kingdom of God and his righteousness?

There are facts which lessen the force of this inference. Every well-regulated mind naturally shrinks from conversing on topics with which those present have no sympathy. For this reason, some whose hearts are right in the sight of God, are silent on religious themes in the railroad car and at the public gathering. It may be questioned whether this silence does not interfere with the testimony which every blood-bought sinner ought to bear to his Redeemer.

A man's testimony ought not to depend merely on his verbal utterance. His inoffensive, kind, manly bearing ought to mark him as something more than a man of the world. His speech should be in keeping with his profession, and when judiciously uttered in the place of public resort may exert a valuable influence. It ought not to be assumed that this world belongs to the followers of

Satan, and that the followers of Christ are to forego, in their presence, all allusions to his cause and their devotion to it.

The fact that some Christians regard religious conversation as a duty, a taking up of the cross, should not put to silence those who desire to converse on subjects of the deepest interest. The formal, perfunctory utterances of mistaken souls, should not repress the utterances prompted by glowing hearts.

Some persons think that religious conversation should consist in dwelling on the details of one's personal experience. No doubt one may be aided by the experience of another in every department of life; yet there are feelings which form a part of our experience in connection with God and his truth, which we feel ought not to be exposed to view. Hence, it is seldom that a person, rich in spiritual experiences, is disposed to lay bare the secret workings of his heart to the view of others.

Nevertheless, those who love the Lord

ought to speak often to one another. Spiritual truths ought to form themes of discourse among those who are cherishing good hopes of salvation. Especially in the retirement of the fireside should these truths form the subject of discourse among the loving members of the family. The strange reluctance some men have to speak on subjects most dear to their hearts must be overcome.

We are social beings. We are to give play to our social sympathies. The joyous affections of our nature are increased by social intercourse with those we love. Our religious emotions, in like manner, will be increased in power. Hence, the duty of social worship. If friends meet to increase their interest in objects to which they are attached, much more should Christians meet and mingle their devotions that they may become more devout.

The usual forms of social worship are family worship and the prayer meeting. It would seem that there should be no need of urging the duty of household prayer, but it is frequently neglected. When not neglected it often degenerates into a mere form. If there is an interesting scene or act, it is that of a family—father, mother, sister, brother—bowing in prayer and thanksgiving before the Giver of every good gift, and the Redeemer of their souls.

The prayer meeting is another form of social worship. It is too often found dull, unprofitable; it should be made interesting and profitable. Instead of formal addresses from "a sense of duty," there should be a free and familiar expression of thought and feeling in regard to the object sought to be attained by the meeting.

If one were a member of a Shakespeare club which held a weekly meeting for a special object, he would make preparation for each meeting. Much more should the attendant of the prayer meeting make preparation of heart and mind. Then would the meeting become an efficient means of spiritual progress.

CHAPTER XVI.

INTELLIGENCE.—COURTESY.

IT is said by some persons that religion has chiefly to do with the heart—with the emotive nature of man. It has to do with his whole nature. It would bring every thought and feeling into subjection to the will of Christ.

Man has an intellectual as well as an emotive nature. It is his duty to use his intellectual powers as they were made to be used. It is his duty to cultivate intelligence as well as love.

Intelligence, mental growth, is cultivated by exercise. God requires men to act soberly and wisely. Sober and wise action in regard to any department of effort, will promote personal improvement. Sobriety is a condition of seeing the truth. The mind cannot see clearly when disturbed by passion. The truth must be seen in relation to an end, in order that means may be wisely adapted for attaining that end.

The sole business of man is to know and to do his duty. In acquiring this idea, he comes in contact with the idea of God, and with his laws. To interpret and apply these laws to the guidance of his life requires thought; and thinking promotes intelligence. The study of duty requires the study of the book made by God, containing truths of the highest order. If the study of the works of a powerful human intellect is adapted to promote mental improvement, much more must the works of the Divine intellect promote mental improvement.

Every one ought to avail himself of all the advantages for mental improvement within his reach. Every Christian ought to be a man of intelligence, even though his educational advantages are small. He has his Bible and the promised aid of the Holy Spirit; he can meditate on truths far higher than those which the highest philosophy has revealed; he can hold communion with the Father of his spirit.

There have not been wanting examples of high intelligence developed by the study of the Bible and the practice of duty. That the examples are so few may be owing to the fact that the duty of cultivating intelligence is not understood.

We are commanded to be courteous. Obedience to this command includes a right use of the body as well as of the mind. The condition of the mind is expressed by voice and action. There should be a suitable correspondence between the condition and the expression.

The meekness and gentleness of Christ, which should be possessed by every one of his followers, are not expressed by the rough, uncouth gesture, and the loud, harsh voice. Love to one's neighbor is not properly expressed by stiff reserve and an aspect of indifference. Right feelings, with their appropriate expression, make a polite man. There are certain conventional usages which form a part of the commonly received code of politeness, and which can ordinarily be acquired only by those who have peculiar social advantages; but these forms are not essential to courteousness. A man's muscles may be rigid; yet if he love his neighbor as himself, his manner will be courteous. Due regard should be paid to the cultivation of kind feelings, and also to their expression. A careless manner in regard to small things often gives pain and interferes seriously with one's influence for good. It has been said that religion is the jewel of the heart, and that good manners are the appropriate setting of the jewel. Intelligence, warm and pure affections, and good manners are necessary in order that the Christian may become "the highest style of man."

CHAPTER XVII.

RELIGIOUS EMOTION.—ZEAL.

IN the opinion of many persons, religion consists chiefly in excited feeling, and the attainment of this state of feeling is the object of religion.

The object of religion is not enjoyment, but a life in perfect conformity to the will of God. The object of religion is not happiness, but holiness.

Religion has to do with our emotive nature as it has to do with our intellectual nature. Religion requires the right exercise of all our powers. The right exercise of all our powers is attended with enjoyment. This is especially true of our emotions and affections.

The right exercise of our emotive nature depends upon the right exercise of our intellectual nature. The heart of the truly religious man is right in the sight of the Lord. His feelings are such as the truth of God is adapted to awaken. The truths of the Bible are adapted to awaken the deepest feelings of the soul. Feelings awakened by correct views of divine truth are rightfully sources of great enjoyment. It is lawful to desire these feelings, not because of the enjoyment attendant on excitement, but because they are the result of the truth of God. The truths of the Bible are adapted to awaken in the mind of the believer, the warmest gratitude, the most fervent love, the most tender sympathy, and the most exalted hopes. These feelings God designed that we should exercise, and he has made their exercise a source of happiness to ourselves and to others. There cannot be too much of this kind of enjoyment. There is no danger of excess in feelings resulting from the correct perception of the divine truth. Mere excitement from sympathy may prove injurious. It may degenerate into fanaticism, which is more injurious than positive infidelity.

Paul did not ask the Lord how he should feel, but what he should do. We should not ask how we can be happy, but how we shall do the will of God. We are to do our duty, and leave our happiness in the hands of God. The happiest men do not make their own happiness an object of direct pursuit; they are those who are most deeply interested in promoting the happiness of others. He who forgets his own happiness in his God-directed efforts for the happiness of others, is the happiest man.

Some men ascribe undue importance to religious zeal; or, rather, seem to think that a burning zeal for the cause of Christ may atone for the neglect of what they regard as inferior duties.

The Bible nowhere teaches that excess in one duty will atone for the neglect of another. When we have done all, we have done only that which it was our duty to do. There can be no excess in genuine zeal.

CHAPTER XVIII.

VAIN SPECULATION.

ALL truth branches out into infinity. There is no truth all of whose connections we can fully grasp. That there are some things which we cannot understand is no reason for rejecting, without examination, those truths which we can understand. We can perceive some truths by the unaided powers of the mind; but we cannot thus perceive all truth. The relations of things in the universe are infinite; but that is no reason why we should not perceive those relations which are within the reach of our powers. We should walk by the light we have, and not spend our time in trying to penetrate the surrounding darkness.

One is walking by the light of a lantern. The light is thrown on the ground before him. He can see clearly where to place each succeeding footstep. He cannot see what lies on the right hand or on the left, or what lies before him. He should not turn away from that light, and vainly endeavor to penetrate the darkness. He should not refuse to walk by that light, because it is limited.

God has given us all the moral light we need. The truths relating to daily duty are exceedingly plain. Some truths are obscure; some things are revealed only in part; some things are not revealed at all. Such are the secret things which belong to God.

Some minds desire to be wise above what is written; they desire to know more of God than he has seen fit to reveal—more than the human mind has the capacity to know. They ask, "How doth God know? How can the acts and the secret thoughts of all beings in the universe be known to Him at the same instant of time? How can God control all things and work all things according to the counsel of his own will, without interfering with man's free agency? Why did God, omnipotent and holy, allow sin to enter the universe?"

To these and similar questions there is but one answer: "We do not know,"—an answer which philosophers are daily compelled to give. Questions plainly beyond the power of the mind to answer, should be dismissed. It is a perversion of the mind to allow it to speculate upon unknowable themes. It injures our power to perceive truth. It leads to a skeptical spirit or habit of mind—a habit detrimental to faith.

Truth does not require the surrender of the mind to authority. The influence of the Bible is favorable to freedom of thought. It requires throughout the normal exercise of mind. It requires that every man should be able to give a reason of the hope that is in him. But it does not favor a skeptical spirit. It is not the friend of philosophy, falsely so called. It does not favor the multiplication of words without knowledge. While it exhorts us to prove all things, and to hold fast that which is good, it teaches that a "Thus saith the Lord," is authority for believing.

Light and grace sufficient for the day are given. This is all that the Christian needs. He has only to follow Christ. It is no concern of his, "What shall this man do?" Christ did not satisfy Peter's curiosity; but gave an answer conveying a delicate reproof: "If I will that he tarry till I come, what is that to thee? Follow thou me." He who honestly desires to know his duty, that he may do it, will always have light sufficient for his guidance.

CHAPTER XIX.

CONFORMITY TO THE WORLD.—PREPARATION FOR HEAVEN.

CHRISTIANS are spoken of by the Apostle as a peculiar people; but it is added that they are peculiar in being zealous of good works. This is by no means an unpleasant peculiarity. So far as a strict regard to duty renders one peculiar, he ought to be peculiar; but factitious peculiarities should be avoided. A peculiar technical phraseology, a neglect of harmless conventional forms, speaking of those without the church as persons to be avoided, are peculiarities which ought not to mark the followers of Jesus. It is true that Christians ought to come out from the world and be separate; but they are not to assume an attitude of antagonism, much less of contempt, toward the world.

Christians should not obtrude their religious profession on others; at the same time they should not conceal it, nor allow those with whom they meet to suppose that they are indifferent to the cause of Christ. The irreverent and profane utterance should not be allowed to pass unnoticed. In what way disapprobation should be expressed, must depend on circumstances. Sometimes it is best expressed by silence. On a certain occasion John Jay dined in Paris with a company of distinguished men, whose conversation was marked by the coarsest infidelity. Jay kept silence, till at length one turned to him, and asked him abruptly: "Do you believe in Christ?" Jay replied, "I thank God that I do." His answer was followed by profound silence on the part of the company. When the conversation was renewed, no allusions were made to infidelity.

Undue conformity to the usages of the world is sometimes practiced under the pretext of gaining influence for good. He who thus departs from religious consistency loses all influence as a religious man.

We must needs associate with other than religious men. We are not to lay aside our Christian character by so doing. Christ mingled freely with all classes of men; still, he was holy, harmless, undefiled, and separate from sinners.

In one sense, our work in this world is to prepare for the world to come. There we are to dwell in the immediate presence of God. Of course we must be perfectly holy. We are increasing in preparation for heaven as we are increasing in holiness.

No details of the future life are given us. We know that to be absent from the body is to be present with the Lord. As we are social beings, heaven will be a social state. As we are active beings, it will be a state of activity. Throughout eternity we shall be engaged in performing the will of God. We know that will is holy, but what its peculiar requirements will be in heaven is not revealed to us. It is enough to know that we shall be like Him; for we shall see him as he is.

It is true that heaven is spoken of as a rest; but it will be a rest, or deliverance, from sin and sorrow, rather than cessation of activity.

It is right and profitable to let our thoughts run forward to the life that is to come; but our main business is preparation for that life by forming our characters after the image of the heavenly. By looking forward to the glorious society and the sinless services of heaven, we may be stimulated to greater diligence in the work of preparation.

Preparation for heaven is preparation for death. If we are Christians, preparation for death has already been made. We are accounted in view of the law as righteous for Christ's sake, and have the promise of being with Christ when we depart hence. Some one may say, "I must have a better preparation for death. I must lead a better life." No doubt every one who is not perfectly holy ought to lead a better life. But will a better life prepare one for death? Are we to avoid sin because we must die? or because the love of Christ constraineth us? The most holy man on earth cannot trust to his own righteousness; he must rely on the perfect righteousness of Christ.

Christians are not to be in bondage through fear of death. Some distress themselves by the anticipation of that solemn hour. They dwell upon the physical accompaniments of death, and the consequences which follow to those who are not saved. They cannot look upon the change without fear.

This bondage can be broken by trusting in Christ. We are to rely upon Him for grace for his daily service, and for grace in a dying hour. If we can trust Him now, we can trust him then.

APPENDIX.

A FEW years ago, Rev. Dr. Curry, then the editor of the *Christian Advocate*, requested me to write him an article on Mr. Bryant's religious character. In consequence of that request, the following article appeared in that paper.

Soon after its publication Mr. Bryant said to me, "You have in your article given the impression that I taught in the Sunday school at Roslyn. I have felt a deep interest in the school, and often visited it and furnished books for it, but I never had a class in it." I asked him if I had made any other mistake in my article. His reply was, "I do not know that you have."

WILLIAM CULLEN BRYANT.

BY AN OLD ACQUAINTANCE.

There is no man living for whom the American people have a higher respect than for William Cullen Bryant. Eleven years ago, when he reached the age of threescore and ten, he was, through the agency of the Century Club, made the recipient of honors such as no other man has received. Since then, on many occasions, his fellow citizens have testified, in the most emphatic manner, their appreciation of him as a poet, a journalist, and a man. His public life, though he has never sought or held a political office, is well known. You ask me to furnish your readers with some account of his religious and social life.

To the best of my knowledge and belief, Mr. Bryant has but one life. There is no duality about him. He has not a public life and a private life. He has not a secular and a religious life. As a member of the family, as a citizen, as a poet, and as a journalist, he has but one life, and that, I am confident, is a thoroughly religious life. The same principles control his actions at all times. His life aim is to do right—to do the will of God.

I do not assume that every conscientious, upright man is a religious, that is, a Christian man. There are men of strict integrity who are not followers of Christ. We have abundant reason for believing that Mr. Bryant is a follower of Christ—that he possesses the faith which works by love and purifies the heart.

It is with no small reluctance that I speak on this topic. You will detect the association which brings to mind an anecdote of a distinguished New England divine of a former generation. A young zealot abruptly asked him, "Do you think you have any religion?" "None to speak of," was the reply. I am led to overcome my reluctance by the thought that it will carry joy to thousands of Christians of every name to know that he whom they honor as a poet, journalist, and patriot, has obtained a like precious faith with them, through the righteousness of God and our Saviour Jesus Christ.

For the proof of Mr. Bryant's religious character we must look to his deeds. He is not a man of professions.

When he resides at Roslyn, during the summer months, he attends the Presbyterian church. He is a regular partaker of the Sacrament of the Lord's Supper; he is a teacher in the Sunday school. The Rev. Dr. Ely, late pastor of the church, said, "Whoever is absent from church on account of cold, or heat, or rain, Mr. Bryant is not absent; he is always in his place in the church and in the Sunday-school."

Partaking of the Lord's Supper is not in itself proof of union to Christ by a living faith. It may be regarded as a meritorious act, contributing to salvation. But in the present case, the act is an evidence of faith. The intense sincerity of Mr. Bryant is well known. It pervades his life. He always says what he means. He has written that only which he has seen, felt, or fully believed. His professions are always in accordance with the truth. He is well acquainted with the theory of the Communion as held by the Presbyterian Church. He knows what is implied in the act of partaking. Hence, it follows that he has exercised the penitence and faith of which the act of communing is the most emphatic profession.

The highest proof of Christian character is the tenor of one's daily life. Mr. Bryant's daily life illustrates the true idea of the Christian life—a life recognizing the will of God as the rule of action, and the merits of Christ as the sole ground of a hope in heaven.

On a certain occasion a friend asked how, with his love of the beautiful, he could give so large a portion of his time and energy to a political journal, which must bring him in contact with uncongenial men, and with themes by no means poetical. His reply brought to mind the following passage from Milton: "It is manifest with what small willingness I endure to interrupt no less hopes than these, and to leave calm and pleasing solitariness to embark upon a troubled sea of noises and hoarse disputes, put from beholding the bright countenance of truth in the quiet of delightful studies; but were it the meanest underservice, if God, by his secretary, conscience, enjoin it, it were sad for me if I should draw back."

Though Mr. Bryant cannot be said to have any religion "to speak of," yet, in the course of an acquaintance of about forty years, the writer has seen him in circumstances leading him to express the profoundest conviction of the sympathy of Christ, and his entire reliance upon Christ for salvation.

In regard to the great change that awaits us all, the following lines from one of his most beautiful poems express, for the most part, the habitual state of his mind :

> "I mark the joy, the terror, yet these within my heart
> Can neither wake the dread nor the longing to depart ;
> And in the sunshine streaming on quiet wood and lea,
> I stand and calmly wait till the hinges turn for me."

You ask me to speak of his social life. With it multitudes are acquainted. He has a very large circle of acquaintances, and enjoys their society. Probably large gatherings are not as much to his taste as is the domestic circle. His intimacies, it is understood, are especially among artists; but he is a lover of good men in every department of life. He does not abound in professions of interest, and is not given to vigorous hand-shaking. When he quietly says, "I am happy to see you," one may feel assured that the words express the exact truth.

In former years it was the fashion of some to speak of him as cold ; and perhaps Mr. Lowell's intimation that he preferred mountains to men, may have given countenance to that manner of speaking. I think it quite probable that, if one should meet him in a rail-car, or some public place, and should utter his name in a manner adapted to awaken the suspicion that he wished to make known his acquaintance with the poet, he might meet with a reception that would bear the epithet noticed above. One such fact would not be sufficient for the formation of a theory. The depth of Mr. Bryant's emotive nature is shown in his poems. These are the transcripts of his character. Some of them could be written only by one who has the capacity for intense affection. These poems are not numerous. Some cases are not strong in proportion to the number of the witnesses.

While God has chosen the poor, rich in faith, as heirs of his kingdom, yet he does not leave himself without witnesses among those on whom he has bestowed large measures of genius and intellectual power. Pascal, Newton, Butler, Milton, Cowper, Bryant, are among the gifted ones who are prepared to crown the Redeemer as Lord of all.

www.ingramcontent.com/pod-product-compliance
Lightning Source LLC
Chambersburg PA
CBHW031343160426
43196CB00007B/717